EAST INDIA COMPANY IN INDIA : FIRST PERIOD (1600 - 1756) TOWNS, FORTRESSES, AND FACTORIES

GOLU KUMAR

Contents

CHAPTER ONE

India in the year 1600. 2. The Commercial and Social Life of the British in Surat and Masulipatam, 1612–1638 3. Madras' Rise and Development, 1639–1680: Portuguese and Dutch Neighbors 4. In 1686, there was British rule and a representative government. 5. Mixed Corporation of Native Americans and Europeans, 1688 6. Slavery and the Indian Slave Trade. 7. Hughly, Madras, Surat, and Bombay. 8. The Great Mogul's collision, 1686–1700. 9. Domestic Management, 1700–1746, 10. Wars were fought in Southern India from 1746 to 1756 against France. 11. Calcutta's Black Hole in June 1756.

The rise of British rule is a side note.

The rise of British rule in India is a problem in history. A single association of British traders established factories that grew into fortresses, and governed native towns which became the capitals of a British empire. The march of events is without a parallel in the annals of the world. In 1600 the East India Company obtained from Queen Elizabeth a charter of exclusive rights to trade in the Eastern seas. In 1612 it established its first factory at Surat. In 1639 it began to build a fortified factory at Madras, whilst a Hindu population of weavers and other manufacturers grew up by its side. Before the beginning of the eighteenth century, before Queen Anne ascended the throne of Great Britain, the British settlements at Madras,

Bombay, and Calcutta had each a fortress and a town. How Hindu and Mohammedan populations were ruled by British traders will be told in the present chapter. How the British traders acquired provinces and established an empire belongs to the after chapters.

[Side note: the Great Mogul was from Northern India.]

§1. In 1600 the whole of Northern India was under the dominion of a Mohammedan sovereign, known as the Great Mogul. His revenues and armies were the marvels of Europe. His empire extended from the mountains of Cashmere to the Bay of Bengal, from the Himalayas slopes to the Deccan tableland. It covered large Hindu populations and many Hindu principalities, for throughout this vast area the Great Mogul was the sovereign lord of all, the emperor, the Padishah.

[Sidenote: SOUTHERN INDIA: Mohammedan Sultans and Hindu Rajas.] South of the Mogul empire was the Deccan or "south." The country was a _terra incognita_ to Europeans. The interior had been conquered by Mohammedan invaders from the north and distributed into kingdoms under Sultans, who formed a barrier against the Moguls. East and west were hills and jungles stretching to the sea, mostly held by Hindu Rajas who were hostile alike to the Sultans and the Great Mogul. Mohammedan rule, however, had never as yet extended further south than the river Kistna. The whole region from the Kistna to Cape Comorin--sometimes known as the "Peninsula"--was under the dominion of Hindu Rajas.

[Sidenote: Portuguese fortresses.]

The western coast of the Deccan and Peninsula was dotted with Portuguese fortresses, mounted with cannon, and garrisoned by Portuguese soldiers. The Portuguese had made their way to India round the Cape of Good Hope about the end of the fifteenth century, and for a hundred years had been building factories in the territories of Hindu Rajas, and converting them into fortresses. Nothing of the kind would have been allowed by the Great Mogul, or by the Sultans of the Deccan, but the Portuguese had persuaded the Hindu Rajas that they would help and protect them, and the Rajas never saw the danger until the fortresses were bristling with cannon and opposition was useless. The Portuguese capital was seated on the island of Goa, about halfway between Surat and Comorin, and was a center of the Catholic religion as well as of Portuguese trade.

[1] [Sidenote: British traders at Surat.]

§2. British merchants in the service of the East India Company would gladly have traded on the same sea-board, known as Malabar's coast, but they were shut out by the Portuguese fortresses. Accordingly, they sailed further northward and tried to get a footing in the Mogul port of Surat. This port was a center of the Mohammedan religion and an emporium of Mogul trade. It was the starting point for all pilgrims going to Mecca and the point to which they returned when their pilgrimage was over. It was the rendezvous of Mogul merchants who despatched ships to the Persian Gulf and the Red Sea and sent goods overland to the great capitals of the Mogul empire--Agra, Delhi, and Lahore.

[Sidenote: British defeat the Portuguese.]

At Surat, however, the British were thwarted by the Portuguese. The Nawab of Surat was told that the British were pirates. The merchants of Surat were threatened with the capture of their ships if they had any dealings with the British. Fighting was the only way of meeting the difficulty. Accordingly the British attacked a Portuguese fleet outside the bar of Surat. The news of the battle and the roar of cannon brought the Nawab, the merchants, and half the population of Surat to the seashore. The British sunk or burnt several Portuguese ships until the residue of the fleet steered back to Goa. The Moguls were fascinated by the victory. They saw that the British had not only superior strength on their side but Allah and kismet. The Nawab of Surat feasted the conquerors in his tents on the sands, and the Surat merchants eagerly bought British cargoes and supplied Indian commodities to the brave men who had beaten the Portuguese.

[Sidenote: British factory at Surat, 1612.]

In 1612 the British set up a factory at Surat in a large Indian house, with warehouses and offices below and chambers and refection-rooms above. It was a London establishment transferred to a Mohammedan seaport. The British merchants, factors, and writers lodged and boarded together like members of one family. Native brokers or banyans were employed to buy cotton goods, silks, indigo, and other Indian commodities; whilst public auctions were held in the factory for the sale of British broadcloths, glass, and cutlery, especially sword-blades, and also for the sale of lead, copper, quicksilver, and other European commodities. The spirit of enterprise was as busy amongst the British as in after years. One factor urged the Company to send ships up the river Indus and open up trade with Central Asia; whilst another tried to persuade the Great Mogul to lay down leaden pipes from the river Jumna to the city of Ajmere, a distance of more than two hundred miles, to convey drinking-water to the imperial palace in the heart of Rajputana.

[Sidenote: Factory life.]

In those early days, no British ladies were allowed to reside in India. If a servant of the Company happened to be married he was obliged to leave his wife in England. The "English House," as it was called, was thus a bachelor establishment, without ladies, but not without Surat punch or Persian wine. An English chaplain read prayers every morning and evening and preached two sermons on Sundays. An English surgeon attended to the sick factors, and the Mogul authorities and other grandees often applied for his services, thus enabling him to promote the Company's interests on more than one important occasion. The chief of the factory was known as the President, but all business was transacted by the President with the help of four or five senior merchants, who met twice a week in council. This management of affairs by a President in the Council has survived the lapse of nearly three centuries. To this day the government of presidencies and the vice-royalty of India are in each case carried on by a President in Council.

[Sidenote: Foreign guests.]

Within a few years, the "English House" at Surat was well known to all European sea captains and voyagers. Not only British travelers, but Italians, Germans, and Frenchmen, were heartily welcomed by the honest factors at Surat. All were impressed with the order and regularity of the establishment, in which decorum and discipline were as strictly maintained as in Leadenhall Street or the Cheape. But when working hours were over the grave men of business proved to be convivial Britons of the old-fashioned type, and on Friday evenings especially, all the married men met together to drink the health of their absent wives to the detriment of their own. Foreign guests who could not speak the English tongue were in no want of amusement. In 1638 a young gentleman from Holstein, named Mandelslo, spent some months in the "English House," and passed the time very pleasantly, visiting the ships at anchor outside the bar of the river Tapty, and hearing the latest news of Europe from sea-captains versed in many languages, or wandering down the row of banyans' shops, which often contained as much wealth, hidden under dirt and squalor, as the houses of London merchants and goldsmiths. On Sundays, after the sermon, the factors carried off their guest to their gardens outside Surat, where they all shot at butts, and were regaled with fruit and conserves.

[Sidenote: British and Moguls.] The European gentlemen at Surat were always polite to Mohammedan grandees and were generally politely treated in return, except perhaps at the custom-house. British sailors and ill-mannered Englishmen would, however, occasionally show a contempt for Asiatics, which the President could not always restrain. British interlopers on the high seas set the Company's charter in defiance, and carried on a lawless trade, plundering the Mohammedan pilgrim ships and ill-treating the passengers. The Mogul authorities insisted that the Company's servants were to blame, and would listen to no explanation, but sent large bodies of Mogul soldiery to environ the "English House," and stop all trade, cutting off all food and water until a sufficient fine or ransom had been paid.

[Sidenote: Trade on the eastern coast.]

About 1620 the East India Company established another factory at Masulipatam on the eastern side of India. The Hindus along the coast of Coromandel were famous for painting muslins and calicoes, and there was a growing demand for such goods amongst the eastern islands, whilst valuable cargoes of nutmegs and other spices could be obtained in exchange. But Masulipatam was seated in the Mohammedan territory. A Sultan of the Deccan, reigning at Golconda, had extended his dominion eastward to the coast of Coromandel and established the port of Masulipatam for the importation of horses from the Persian Gulf. The traders at the British factory were therefore cramped and worried by the Mohammedan authorities, and yearned to settle on the territories of some Hindu Raja further south, where they could fortify a factory and mount it with British cannon without the interference of local authorities.

[Sidenote: British territory and fortress at Madras, 1639.]

§3. In 1639 a British merchant named Day bought a strip of territory on the Coromandel coast, about 300 miles to the south of Masulipatam. It was within the dominions of a Hindu Raja and was about six miles long and one mile inland. It included a small island, which faced the sea and was defended on the land side by a river. Mr. Day agreed to pay the Raja a rent of 500_l._ a year in native coins known as pagodas, and the transaction was duly engraved on a plate of gold. A factory of brick was built upon the island, mounted with cannon, and called Fort St. George. The Raja was perfectly content. He was too glad to get a rent of 500_l._ a year to raise any difficulty as regards fortifications or cannon.

[Sidenote: Fort St. George and Black Town.]

This factory was the germ of the city of Madras, on the coast of Coromandel. Weavers, washers, painters, and hosts of other Hindu artisans, flocked to the spot and eagerly entered the service of the British, and began to set up their looms and weave, wash, and paint their cotton goods in the open air beneath the trees. Villages of little huts of mud and bamboo soon grew up on the sandy soil to the north of the island and factory. Each avocation formed a caste, which generally had its quarters and its headman. In this manner a Hindu settlement grew up by the side of Fort St. George and was known as Black Town; the whole locality, including Fort St. George and Black Town, was called Madras and was the first territory acquired by the East India Company in India.

[Sidenote: Despotic rule.]

The transition of the British traders from a factory under Mohammedan control to an independent settlement of their own must have been a grateful change. The President and Council at Fort St. George were _de facto_ rulers of the whole settlement, native as well as European, with all the powers of despotic princes and with no interference from without. They acted as a supreme court of judicature for Englishmen in all cases civil and criminal; no Englishman, however, could be condemned to death unless convicted of piracy, which was regarded as the most heinous of crimes. On all other capital charges, the Englishman was sent to England for trial.[2]

[Sidenote: Portuguese and Dutch neighbors.]

Four miles to the south of Fort St. George was the Portuguese town of St. Thomé, but the Portuguese were now friends with the English. Their power was being overshadowed by that of the Dutch, who had founded a town and fortress at Pulicat, nearly thirty miles to the northward of Fort St. George.

[Sidenote: Dutch trade in India.]

The Dutch settlements in India were the outcome of the hostility of Spain. For centuries the Dutch had been the carriers of Europe, from the Mediterranean to the Baltic. In the period which preceded the sixteenth century, they had bought Indian commodities at Genoa, Naples, and Venice. After the Portuguese established trade in India, the Dutch went every year to Lisbon to buy Indian commodities for the European markets. In 1580 they threw off the yoke of Spain and founded the United Provinces. That same year Spain and Portugal were formed into one kingdom under Philip II. In an evil hour for Portuguese interests in India, Philip thought to punish the Dutch by shutting them out of Lisbon. The Dutch revenged themselves by sailing round the Cape and buying what they wanted in the islands of the Eastern Archipelago. In 1600 they built a factory in Java, which grew into the city of Batavia. In 1610 they built a square fort on Pulicat Lake, which grew into the town of Pulicat and threatened to become the capital of Dutch ascendency in India.

[Sidenote: Right and Left Hands.]

The Indian quarter at Madras was almost entirely Hindu. Scarcely a Mohammedan took up his abode within the Company's bounds. Accordingly one of the earliest acts of the President and Council was to divide the streets of Black Town into those of the right and left hand. All over Southern India, the lower castes of Hindus are divided into Right and Left Hands, and yet no one can account for the distinction, or satisfactorily define the respective rights of each Hand. The so-called Hands are, however, intensely jealous of each other. For generations, each Hand in the towns of Southern India has had its streets and its pagoda. At Madras, if one Hand passed in religious procession along the streets of the other hand, or if the members of one Hand chanted Hindu hymns or mantras before the pagoda of the other, a fray would break out in Black Town, which could only be suppressed by British soldiers, and then would be followed by a strike of weavers or painters, or the flight of all the members of one Hand to the Portuguese settlement at St. Thomé. These conflicts, which more than once brought the settlement to the brink of ruin, reached a climax in Governor Pitt's time, as will appear hereafter.

[Sidenote: Mohammedan invasion.]

Meanwhile, the country round about Madras was in a state of turmoil. The Mohammedan army of the Sultan of Golconda was advancing against the Hindu Rajas of the south and formed a camp in the neighborhood. The Raja who had sold the territory to the East India Company fled away to the interior and was never heard of more. The Mohammedan army captured the Portuguese town of St. Thomé, dismantled the walls of the fortress, and carried off the cannon to Golconda; and they would have treated Fort St. George in like fashion, had not the British stoutly resisted, and quieted the Sultan by engaging to pay him the rent which they had previously paid to the Raja.

[Sidenote: Troubles with Dutch and French, 1670.]

About 1670, or some thirty years after the foundation of Madras, the state of affairs was complicated by Charles II.'s unholy alliance with France against the Dutch. A French fleet attacked St. Thomé and drove out the Mohammedans. A Dutch fleet from Pulicat recaptured St. Thomé, drove out the French, and restored the place to the Sultan of Golconda. The British settlement was in sore peril, but in 1674 there was peace between Great Britain and Holland, and the danger was over.

[Sidenote: Increase of population.]

These troubles brought many strangers to Madras, and the population, white and black, was largely increased. Many Portuguese families from St. Thomé took refuge in Madras and added to the strength of the European settlement, known as White Town, by building houses under the protection of the factory guns. The British factors and soldiers of the garrison married the daughters of the Portuguese, much to the horror of the English chaplain of Fort St. George, as the marriages were accompanied by numerous conversions of bridegrooms to the Catholic faith. At the same time, wealthy Hindu traders and bankers began to build substantial houses in Black Town for the sake of British protection. Many invested their money in trading voyages; some acted as brokers or banyans for the supply of Indian commodities to the Company's servants; others bought European goods at the public auctions, and supplied the native dealers up the country.

[Sidenote: Fort St. George, 1670-86.]

§4. Within forty years of the building of the British factory, Madras was the pride and glory of the East India Company. Fort St. George, or White Town, was a European city in miniature. The primitive factory in the center was replaced by a stately mansion with a dome, which was known as the Governor's House, but included a town hall, a council chamber, and sundry offices. It was seated in an open square, having a strong wall along each of its four sides, guards' houses and bastions at each corner mounted with cannon. Outside the fortification were little streets, paved with pebbles, containing about fifty European houses. There was also a Protestant church for the English inhabitants and a Catholic chapel for the Portuguese residents. The whole of White Town was environed by an outer wall, sufficiently fortified to keep off an Indian army. None but Britons, or Europeans under British protection, were permitted to reside in White Town. The garrison consisted of two companies of European soldiers, and a large number of native guards, who were known as peons.

[Sidenote: Hindu town under British rule.]

At this time the population of the native town was estimated at 300,000 souls but was probably half that number, and an attempt was made to introduce something like a representative government. Whenever the Governor and Council desired to know the wishes of the people generally or to act with their consent, they summoned the headmen of castes and consulted them accordingly. Justice, however, was administered by two English gentlemen, who sat twice a week in Black Town in a building known as the Choultry. The Justices of the Choultry tried all offenses and disputes amongst the Hindus, and fined, flogged, or imprisoned at discretion. The old English punishments of the stocks, the pillory, and the gallows were also in full force in Black Town, but no Hindu was executed without the confirmation of the Governor and Council. The Justices of the Choultry were bound by no code of laws; they were simply instructed by the Directors of the Company in England to decide all cases, civil and criminal, according to "equity and good conscience," guided by English law and their own experiences of Hindu customs and usages.[3] A Hindu superintendent of police was appointed under the title of "Pedda Naik," or "elder chief;" and he was bound to maintain a certain number of constables known as peons, and keep the peace of the town. He was expected to prevent theft and burglary, and either recover stolen property or pay the value to the owner. In return, the Pedda Naik was allowed to cultivate a few fields rent-free, and to levy a small octroi duty, or toll, on articles of Hindu consumption.

[Sidenote: Protection of Hindus.]

The main difficulty at Madras was to keep the peace between the European soldiers of the garrison and the Hindu population. Any European soldier who remained outside the Fort at night time was set publicly in the stocks for a whole day. Any European who attempted to get over the Fort walls was imprisoned in irons for one entire month and kept on rice and water. Any soldier who threatened to strike a Hindu was whipped. Any European who took an article out of a shop or bazaar, under the pretense of buying it at his price, was sentenced to pay treble the value to the party aggrieved.

[Sidenote: Question of taxation.]

Another difficulty was to keep the streets of Black Town clean and wholesome. The Governor and Council summoned the heads of castes and proposed to levy a small tax on every house. The heads assented to the measure but offered to carry out the work themselves and to raise the necessary funds in the same way that they levied contributions from their respective castes for defraying the cost of public festivals. All this, however, was a blind on their part to delude the British Governor and Council. Nothing was done by the heads of castes, no money was collected, and the streets were dirtier than ever.

[Sidenote: Contumacy of heads of castes.]

Meanwhile, Madras was threatened by the Sultan of Golconda, and the Directors in England instructed the Governor and Council at Madras to build a wall around Black Town, and meet the cost by levying a small ground rent from each householder. In this case, no difficulty was anticipated. The Hindus might ignore the importance of sanitation, but they could scarcely refuse to contribute towards the defense of their lives and property, to say nothing of their wives and families. The heads of castes, however, raised strong objections but found that the Governor was bent on carrying out the orders of the Court of Directors. The heads of castes were told that the rents must be paid and that those who refused to pay must be prepared to sell their houses and leave the British settlement. At this threat, they all promised to pay but secretly prepared for a general uprising.

[Sidenote: Hindu rebellion, 1686.]

Suddenly, one Sunday morning, the 3rd of January, 1686, it was known in Fort St. George that the Hindu population of Black Town was rebelling in Asiatic fashion. Under the orders of the heads of castes, the Hindu servants of the Company had thrown up their duties, bazaar dealers had shut up their shops, and provisions and grain were kept out of the town. The Governor in Fort St. George sent a detachment of the British garrison to guard the entrances to Black Town and suppress the tumult. The proclamation was made by beat of a drum that unless the heads submitted before sunset, their houses would be pulled down on the following morning, the sites sold by auction, and the rebels and their families banished forever. Hindus who failed to return to their duties would be discharged from the Company's service; dealers who kept their shops closed would be heavily fined and all their goods confiscated. These peremptory orders had the desired effect. The heads of castes seemed to be completely cowed. Before sunset, they appeared at the Fort and begged pardon for their rebellion, and were told to put an end to the tumult in Black Town.

[Sidenote: Wholesome despotism.]

The next morning the heads of castes returned to the Fort and presented a petition, begging to be relieved from the payment of the ground rent. Each man was asked in turn whether he would leave the town, and each, in turn, said that he would submit, and then the whole body declared with one voice that they would not pay the tax. The proclamation was at once made by beat of drum that the orders of Sunday would be immediately put in execution. The Hindus bent to the storm. They saw that they were at the mercy of their British rulers. The shops were opened, provisions were brought into the town, and all the artisans and servants of the Company returned to their duties. The ground rents were collected without demur, and later on, the scavenger tax was raised without difficulty.

[Sidenote: Mayor, aldermen, and burgesses, 1688.]

§5. When the news of these disturbances reached England, the Directors in Leadenhall Street, or rather their once celebrated chairman, the great Sir Josiah Child, devised a scheme for rendering municipal taxation acceptable to the native population. A charter was obtained from James II. for founding a corporation in Madras, consisting of a mayor, twelve aldermen, and sixty burgesses; but it was suggested by the Court of Directors that the heads of Hindu castes, as well as Britons, might be appointed aldermen and burgesses, and it was hoped that the corporation would be willing to tax themselves and the inhabitants generally, for keeping the town clean, improving the public health, building a guild-hall and hospitals, and establishing schools for teaching the English tongue to Hindus, Mohammedans, and other Indian children. Before the Governor and Council at Madras could offer a single suggestion, they received instructions to cut and dried. The mayor and three senior aldermen were always to be covenanted British servants of the East India Company, and they alone were to be Justices of the Peace. The remaining nine might belong to any nationality, and included Portuguese, Hindu, and Jewish merchants having dealings with the Company at Madras. Thirty burgesses were named in the charter, but they were all Englishmen;

and the remainder were to include the heads of all the castes, to induce the whole of the Hindu inhabitants to contribute cheerfully to the public works already specified. The mayor and aldermen were to wear red silk gowns, and the burgess's white silk gowns and maces were to be carried before the mayor. In a word, all the paraphernalia of an English municipality in the seventeenth century were sent to Madras to be adopted by the new corporation.

[Sidenote: Corporation festivities.]

The new municipality was inaugurated with much pomp and ceremony in 1688, the year of the Glorious Revolution. The Governor of Madras was outside the corporation, but the mayor and three senior aldermen were members of the council. On Saturday, the 29th of September, 1688, the Governor received the mayor, aldermen, and burgesses in the council chamber at Fort St. George. The members of the new corporation then took the oaths and sat down to a corporation dinner; and after a while, they all marched to the town hall in their several robes, with the maces before the mayor. Nothing, however, is said about the heads of castes, and nothing more about the burgesses.

[Sidenote: Failure of municipal rule.]

The mayor and aldermen were to be a Court of Record, with power to try all causes, criminal and civil, in a summary way, according to "equity and good conscience," and such laws and orders as might be made by the Company. The corporation was authorized to levy taxes for building a guild hall, a public jail, and a schoolhouse for teaching English, arithmetic, and merchants' accounts to Indian children, and for payment of the necessary salaries. Henceforth, two aldermen sat as justices of the Choultry; but the corporation raised no tax and founded no institution, and eventually died out from sheer want of vitality.

[Sidenote: Slavery under Hindu rule.]

§6. All this while the slave trade was an institution in Madras, and indeed, throughout Southern India. In most of the Hindu kingdoms of the Peninsula, the farm laborers were slaves or serfs attached to the soil; they were probably aboriginal populations who had been reduced to slavery by their conquerors. Prisoners of war, male and female, were also compelled to serve the conquerors as domestic servants and treated as slaves of the family.

[Sidenote: Mohammedan slavery.]

When Turks and Afghans introduced Mohammedan rule, slavery was recognized, but Hindu slaves might raise their condition by embracing Islam, and the converts might become important personages in the household, and married female members of the family. The favorites of a grandee or Sultan might even marry a daughter, and rise to the rank of steward of the household or minister of state, like Joseph in the court of the Pharaohs.

[Sidenote: Mogul restrictions.]

When the Moguls established their dominion over Northern India there was a change for the better. It was a fundamental law of the Moguls that no subject should be enslaved, but only captives taken in war. This law was still enforced when the Moguls became Mohammedans, for they always looked upon the slavery of subjects with horror, whatever might be their race or religion. Foreign slaves, male and female, provided they were not Mohammedans, were sold by private dealers, or in the public bazaar.[4]

[Sidenote: the Portuguese slave trade.]

Unfortunately, the Portuguese and other nations of Europe had not as yet awakened to the iniquity of slavery and the slave trade. During the Portuguese wars in Africa, Moors and Negroes were carried off as prisoners of war and sold as slaves in Lisbon. In India, the Portuguese established depôts for the purchase of slaves. At Goa female slaves were to be found in every Portuguese household, and sometimes were sent into the streets to sell sweetmeats and confectionary, and earn money for their masters in other ways.

[Sidenote: Kidnapping from Bengal.]

For many years large numbers of Hindu slaves were brought from Bengal. The Portuguese had been permitted to build a factory at Hughly, on the river Hooghly, about 120 miles from the sea. During an interval of the civil war, they fortified this settlement and landed numerous cannons, whilst a native town grew up in the neighborhood. Meanwhile, the scum of Goa and other Portuguese towns, chiefly military deserters and apostate monks, had established themselves on the islands near the mouths of the Ganges, built a fleet of galleys, and led the lives of pirates, brigands, and kidnappers. These men were the pest of the Sunderbunds. They scoured the waterways of the delta of the Ganges, carried off whole villages into slavery, and especially delighted in capturing marriage processions, with the bride and bridegroom and all their kinsfolk and acquaintance in the bravery of silks and jewels. The Portuguese at Hughly were base enough to deal with these villains, to buy the poor wretches who had been kidnapped, and to ship them to Goa, where they were sold as slaves at the daily auctions on the Exchange, together with other commodities from all parts of the world. The rascally kidnappers at the mouths of the Ganges, and the pious traders at Highly, alike quieted their consciences by baptizing their victims and boasting of having saved their souls from hell.

[Sidenote: Vengeance of the Great Mogul.]

Such a state of things aroused the Great Mogul to take action. The very existence of a Portuguese fortress and cannon within his dominions had given mortal offense, and this unholy slave trade sealed the fate of the Portuguese at Highly. The settlement was environed by a Mogul army. There was a rush of ladies and children to the shipping, but the river was low and the vessels ran aground. There was absolutely no way of escape; all provisions were cut off, and the Portuguese were starved into surrender. Five or six hundred prisoners, many of noble birth, were sent to Agra. Some saved their lives by turning Mohammedans; others, mostly priests, perished as martyrs; the choicest of the lads and maidens were sent to the palace of the Great Mogul, and the remainder were distributed amongst the mansions of the Mohammedan grandees. For generations, afterward, the doom of the Portuguese at Hughly was likened to the Babylonian captivity of the Hebrews.

[Sidenote: Slave trade at Madras.]

Highly was captured in 1632. Seven years later the British built their factory at Madras, on the coast of Coromandel. At every Portuguese settlement in Southern India, the slave trade was still in full swing, for the sway of the Great Mogul had only been extended over the northern part of the Deccan, and was as yet far away from the Peninsula. Accordingly, the British traders at Madras connived at the exportation of slaves by sea. Some restraints, however, were placed upon kidnapping by insisting on the registration of every slave bought or sold in Madras, together with the names of the seller and purchaser, so that the information might be given in the event of any inquiry by kinsfolk or acquaintance, and also that a fee might be levied on the registration of every slave.

[Sidenote: Great Mogul conquers the Deccan.]

In 1688 the British rulers of Madras abolished the slave trade by public proclamation. The Great Mogul, the once famous Aurangzeb, was engaged in conquering the Sultans of the Deccan. Unlike his predecessors, Aurangzeb was a bigoted Sunni or a zealous believer in the four Caliphs who succeeded Mohammed. The Sultans of the Deccan were Shiahs who damned the first three Caliphs as usurpers and swore that Ali, and Ali only, the son-in-law of the Prophet, the husband of Fatima and the father of Hassan and Hosein, was the rightful successor of Mohammed. Under such circumstances, Aurangzeb was impelled by pious zeal for the interest of the Sunni religion to conquer and slay the heretic Sultans of the Deccan and annex their dominions to the Mogul empire. He next prepared to march his army further south into the Peninsula, with the view of conquering the Hindu Rajas and compelling their idolatrous subjects to accept the religion of the Koran.

[Sidenote: Stoppage of the slave trade.]

The British at Madras were greatly alarmed at the threatened approach of the Great Mogul. They were naturally afraid of sharing the fate of the Portuguese at Highly. Accordingly, they abolished the slave trade by proclamation, and sent numerous petitions to Aurangzeb, tendering their submission to the Great Mogul, praising his imperial majesty to the skies, imploring his protection as though he had been another Cyrus or Darius, and engaging to pay the old rent of 500_l._ per annum in pagodas. Matters were finally arranged, but it is grievous to add that the pious Aurangzeb was not so careful of the welfare of the Hindus as his liberal and tolerant predecessors. He preferred the laws of Mohammed to those of his Mogul ancestor, Chenghiz Khan; and within a few years, the slave trade at Madras was as brisk as ever.

[Sidenote: British toleration.]

§7. The Mogul conquest of the Sultans of the Deccan drove many Mohammedans to settle at Madras. The British traders protected the lives and property of Hindus and Mohammedans and permitted them to worship as they pleased. In the early days, the Directors had repeatedly pressed their servants at Madras to convert the Hindu worshippers of idols to the truths of Christianity, and no one in the British Isles seems to have doubted the possibility or expediency of the work. The British traders at Madras, however, deprecated any interference whatever. They described a terrible riot that broke out at St. Thomé because of some interference with a Hindu procession, and they urged that the frays between the Right and Left Hands were sufficient proof that it was best to leave the Hindus alone. As for Mohammedans, they were the subjects of the Great Mogul, and interference with the dominant religion in India was out of the question.

[Sidenote: Flourishing private trade.]

During the latter years of the seventeenth century, the British settlement at Madras had grown into a principality, independent, and self-contained. At the same time, it presented rare attractions to traders, Asiatic as well as European. The Company's servants were paid very small salaries but were allowed the privilege of private trade in the eastern seas, so long as they paid customs and did not interfere with the European trade. Every Company's servant in Madras, from the Governor to the youngest writer, engaged more or less in trading ventures. The number of traders was swelled by private individuals who came from England, under the license of the Court of

Directors; as well as by Hindu, Mohammedan, and Armenian merchants, who often took shares with the Company's servants. Moreover, this private trade increased the demand for European commodities which were sold by public auction in Fort St. George and swelled the revenue of the East India Company which was derived from the sea customs.

[Sidenote: Decay of Surat.]

Meanwhile, the British situation at the Mogul port of Surat had become intolerable. The religious fanaticism of Aurangzeb had stirred up hatred and discontent amongst Christians and Hindus. The factors at the English House were more oppressed than ever. On the north, their trade was cut off by the Rajput princes of Western Hindustan, who were revolting against the Great Mogul and stopping the caravans between Surat and Agra. On the south, they were exposed to the Mahrattas of the Western Deccan, who attacked and plundered Surat, and would have plundered the English House had not the factors surreptitiously landed some cannon, and called in the British sailors from the shipping, and manfully beaten off their assailants.

[Sidenote: Bombay, 1661-85.]

Fortunately, the British had taken possession of the island of Bombay, which Charles the Second had obtained from the King of Portugal as part of the dowry of the Infanta Catharine, and made over to the East India Company. Bombay was nearly two hundred miles to the south of Surat and hedged around by the Mahrattas, but being an island it was well protected and included both a fortress and a town. Moreover, it had a magnificent harbor, and the valuable trade with the Persian Gulf, the Red Sea, and Mozambique could be better carried on from this harbor than over the bar of Surat at the mouth of the river

Tasty. Accordingly, the East India Company secretly resolved on leaving Surat forever and remove the British factors and their trade to the island of Bombay.

[Sidenote: Bengal trade, 1640-85.]

In Bengal the East India Company had established a factory at Highly, hard by the dismantled Portuguese fortress; but were exposed to so much insolence and extortion from the Mogul authorities that they were prepared to leave Bengal rather than tamely submit to further oppression. The trade was enormously profitable and had helped to defray the cost of the fortifications at Madras and Bombay. Saltpeter had been in large demand ever since the breaking out of the civil war between Charles the First and his parliament. Raw silk and opium were equally marketable, and all three products could be brought from Patna to Highly by the river Ganges. At Dacca, the old capital of Bengal to the eastward of the Ganges, muslins were manufactured of so fine a texture that a piece sufficient for a dress might be passed through a wedding ring; and every young lady in the British Isles who aspired to be a bride was equally anxious to be led to the altar in a cloud of Dacca muslin. Aurangzeb, however, stopped the supply of saltpeter, because the Sultan of Turkey complained that it was used by Christians in their wars against true believers; whilst the Nawab of Bengal, who resided at Dacca, was most overbearing, and on one occasion ordered that Mr. Job Charnock, the chief of the Highly factory, should be imprisoned and scourged, and his orders were obeyed by the Highly officials.

[Sidenote: Plans of Sir Josiah Child, 1685.]

§8. Sir Josiah Child, the chairman of the Court of Directors, was endowed with real political genius, but he was imperious and headstrong. He resolved to make war upon the Great Mogul, and compel him to make reparation for the misdeeds of the Nawab of Bengal, and to cede sufficient territory for the establishment of a fortress and a town corresponding to the settlements at Madras and Bombay. He proposed to coerce the Great Mogul by sending out the Company's cruisers from Bombay to capture the Mogul ships going to Mecca until Aurangzeb came to terms. He also persuaded James II. to send a Royal fleet to Bengal to ensure the success of his scheme. Should his plans fail, should Aurangzeb prove obstinate and impracticable, it was intended to ally with the Raja of Arakan, on the eastern side of the Bay of Bengal, and promise to help him in his wars against the Great Mogul, provided he ceded the required territory at Chittagong. In short, Sir Josiah Child proposed to overawe the Mogul and establish British trade with India on a lasting basis for the future using three great fortresses--one at Madras, a second at Bombay, and a third in Bengal or at Chittagong.

[Sidenote: Elements of mischief.]

Unfortunately, Sir Josiah Child was unable to cope with the craft and capacity of Aurangzeb. That keen-witted sovereign had spies in all directions and was gifted with such a power of divining what was going on that he was often suspected of employing supernatural agency. Meanwhile, Sir Josiah Child was maintaining such profound secrecy that no Englishman on the Bengal side knew what was going on at Surat or Bombay, and no Englishman on the Bombay side knew what was going on in the Bay of Bengal, whilst the British at Madras knew nothing whatever of the plans in operation.

[Sidenote: Blunders and disasters.]

The blundering that followed was most disastrous. Whilst the Company's cruisers were capturing Mogul ships as lawful prizes, Aurangzeb drew the Surat factors into his clutches, and threatened to put them to death unless the prizes were restored and vast sums paid by way of ransom. Meanwhile, the Royal fleet arrived in Bengal, and made its way up the river Hughly, under the command of a certain Captain Heath, who would listen to no advice and regarded Asiatics with contempt, whilst he was ready to make war on anybody. He brought away Mr. Job Charnock and the British factors from Hughly, with all their goods and records. He captured all the Mogul ships he encountered in the Hooghly river. He bombarded a Mogul town at the mouth of the river. Meanwhile, the Nawab of Bengal was in a panic of fear at Dacca, willing to make any terms provided only that the terrible admiral would leave Bengal and solemnly promise never to return.

[Sidenote: A hot-headed admiral.]

The Royal fleet sailed to Arakan and frightened the Raja into a state of utter bewilderment. The Raja could make nothing of the offer of the admiral to help him against the Great Mogul, nor of the demand for the cession of Chittagong, and he naturally vacillated, prevaricated, and procrastinated. The admiral was blind with rage and mortification and would have captured Chittagong by force of arms, but the place was too strong for him. Accordingly, he sailed away to Madras in a towering fury, and landed Mr. Charnock and the British factors at Madras, swearing that he had heard nothing but deceit and lies since he first entered the Bay of Bengal.

[Sidenote: Humiliation.]

The East India Company submitted to the Great Mogul, but the great Josiah Child must have found it a bitter pill. The prizes were restored, a vast fine was paid, and pardon was humbly implored before the Surat factors were restored to liberty.

[Sidenote: Calcutta founded, 1690.]

Meanwhile, the Moguls had learned to respect the British. The fugitives from Highly were invited to return to Bengal and permitted to purchase a strip of land on the eastern bank of the Hooghly river, about twenty miles nearer the sea than their old factory. It was three miles long and one mile inland and included the three native villages of Chutanutti, Govindpore, and Kali Ghat, which grew into a native town resembling that of Madras. Later on, the Hindus round about revolted against Mogul oppression, and the British took advantage of the general alarm to convert their factory into a fortress and give it the name of Fort William, in honor of the Prince of Orange. The native settlement was known by the name of Calcutta, after the village of Kali Ghat, or the "landing place of the goddess Kali." Thus the dream of Josiah Child was realized, and British trade in India was protected by three fortresses and three towns--Madras, Bombay, and Calcutta.

[Sidenote: Indian calm, 1700-40.]

From the end of the seventeenth century to the middle of the eighteenth the Company's settlements were for the most part shut out from the Indian world. The British had learned their lesson and kept quiet, and the Moguls were busy fighting the Mahrattas and left them very much alone. The Mogul conquests in the Deccan were made over to a Mogul Viceroy known as the Nizam, whilst those in the eastern Peninsula round about Madras were placed in charge of a Nawab who was known as the Nawab of the Carnatic. Meanwhile, the Moguls kept the Mahrattas quiet by the payment of a yearly black-mail known as chout, or "_chauth_," which was reckoned at one-fourth of the land revenue but was often commuted for a lump sum. Thus

India was to all outward appearance in a state of calm, but it was the calm that precedes a storm.

[Sidenote: Typical Madras Governors.]

§9. Although the administration of Madras was carried on by a Governor and Council yet each Governor had a strong personal influence and individuality. Two of these Governors, an Englishman, and a Scotchman may be brought under notice as types of all.

[Sidenote: Governor Pitt, 1698-1709.]

THOMAS PITT, the grandfather of the Earl of Chatham, was Governor of Madras from 1698 to 1709. In 1702 the Nawab of the Carnatic was staying at St. Thomé, trying to squeeze some 50,000_l_. out of the British at Madras. He boasted loudly of his friendship with the British whilst his troops were plundering their outlying villages. He was entertained at dinner with great pomp at Fort St. George and gratified with presents, but shortly afterward he environed the whole settlement with his army. Pitt held out for months, getting his supplies by sea. At last, Pitt offered two or three thousand pounds in rupees, and a peace was patched up, and the Nawab went away.

[Sidenote: Imperious rule.]

Governor Pitt was as lofty and mysterious in his way as his illustrious grandson. He was much irritated by a protracted quarrel between the Right and Left Hands. He set up stones to mark the boundaries between the streets, but they were carried away at night time. The bulk of the Right Hands fled to St. Thomé, and the Hindu populations in all the country roundabout were in great commotion. Pitt threatened to send a body of European soldiers to St. Thomé and put the deserters to the sword. During this crisis, the Mogul officer at St. Thomé turned the malcontents out of the town. They went back to Madras submissive and crestfallen and begged to be forgiven. From this time, however, the distinction between the Right and Left Hands was abolished as far as the streets were concerned, and all streets were opened to both Hands. But the old strife is still burning in the hearts of the Hindus of Southern India. They can be prevented from fighting with swords and clubs, but they carry the battle into the law courts, where disputes are frequently brought to a decision as regards the right of either Hand to worship at a particular shrine and in a particular way.[5]

[Sidenote: Hasty tempter.]

Pitt was severe on native offenders. Some thieves went off with boat-loads of cotton goods, and the gunner at Fort St. George was ordered to fire upon them. The thieves escaped, but two peons who connived at the robbery were whipped and put in the pillory, whilst Governor Pitt thrashed the native overseer with his own hands.

[Sidenote: Pitt diamond.]

During the siege of Madras Pitt managed to buy a wonderful diamond from a Golconda jeweler at a small price. After years, he sold it to the Regent of France for 135,000_l._, and it was known as the Pitt diamond. The matter created some scandal at the time, but is now only remembered in connection with Pope's lines:-- "Asleep and naked as an Indian lay, An honest factor stole his gem away."

[Sidenote: Governor Macrae, 1725-30.]

JAMES MACRAE, a Scotch celebrity, was Governor of Madras from 1725 to 1731. He carried out a general survey of Madras and its suburbs for the better collection of the quit-rents and scavenger-tax. The population of Madras numbered 200,000. The expenses of Fort St. George amounted to 20,000_l_. a year, whilst the revenue from the sea customs was under 5,000_l._

[Sidenote: Mayor's Court.]

The Mayor's Court was re-organized in Governor Macrae's time under the charter of 1726. It was to consist of a mayor and nine aldermen for the trial of all civil causes. Seven of the aldermen were to be Englishmen, and the remaining two of any nation provided they were Protestant. The new court was inaugurated in a style that seems inexpressibly absurd in the present day. The new mayor and aldermen were sworn in with much ceremony and then left Fort St. George in a grand procession of soldiers with kettledrums and trumpets, dancing girls with the country music, court attorneys with all the chief gentry on horseback, and passed through Black Town to the Company's garden in the suburbs, where they were received by the Governor and Council and duly _fêted_.

[Sidenote: Breaking up of the Mogul empire.]

Meanwhile, the Mogul empire was breaking up. Aurangzeb died in 1707. Within thirty years after his death the power of the Great Moguls had died out; the name and prestige remained, but very little more. The successors of Aurangzeb were _Roisfainéants_ shut up in palaces with wives and concubines, whilst all real power was exercised by the Ministers of State and the Viceroys of the provinces. In 1738-39 the British at the three Presidencies were startled by the news that Nadir Shah had invaded India with a large Persian army from the north-west, and had plundered the city and palaces of Delhi and carried away the spoil of Northern India. The payment of the Mahratta "chout" was stopped at the Mogul treasury, and armies of Mahratta horsemen were making up the loss by the plunder of the Carnatic and Bengal.

[Sidenote: War with France, 1745.]

§10. In 1745 news reached India that war had been declared between Great Britain and France. This was alarming news for the British traders at Madras, as the French had established a flourishing town and settlement at Pondicherry, on the coast of Coromandel, about a hundred miles to the south of Madras, and a collision might be expected at any moment between the two settlements. Moreover, the Governor of Pondicherry was a certain M. Dupleix, a Frenchman of large capacity and restless ambition, who hated the British with all the ardor of the typical Frenchman of the eighteenth century. The same year a British fleet appeared off the coast of Coromandel and threatened Pondicherry, but the Nawab of the Carnatic declared that he would have no wars between European nations within his territories, and the British fleet sailed away.

[Sidenote: Madras captured, 1746.]

In 1746 a French fleet appeared off Madras, but the Nawab was not inclined to interfere; he had been bought over by M. Dupleix, the French Governor of Pondicherry. The French bombarded Fort St. George; the native inhabitants fled from Madras, and the British inhabitants were carried in triumph to Pondicherry as prisoners of war.

[Sidenote: French defeat the Mogul army.]

The Nawab of the Carnatic affected was very angry at this bombardment of Madras. He demanded that the settlement should be transferred to his authority, and sent an army of 10,000 Moguls to take possession of the town and fortress. To his utter amazement, the army of 10,000 Moguls was utterly routed by a battalion of 800 Frenchmen. From that day it was felt throughout Southern India that no Mogul army could stand against the rapid firing of disciplined Europeans. In 1748 the war between Great

Britain and France was over for a while, and Madras was restored to the British.

[Sidenote: Brilliant success of Dupleix.]

Later on, the death of the Nizam of the Deccan threw the whole country into confusion. Rival kinsmen began to fight for the throne of the province without any reference to the Great Mogul. Dupleix plunged at once into the fray. He saw that a French force might turn the scale of victory, and he moved a French army, under the command of Bussy, to help a victorious candidate as occasion served, without the slightest regard to the rightness or wrongness of his claim. In 1751 he realized his dream of ambition. He had placed a Nizam on the throne at Hyderabad, and he was rewarded with the cession of a territory stretching 600 miles along the coast, for the maintenance of a French standing army. To crown all, he induced the Nizam to appoint him Nawab of the Carnatic; and, despite Dupleix being a Frenchman and a Catholic, the appointment was made under the seal of the Great Mogul. Meanwhile, the British had supported the claim of a Mogul prince named Mohammed Ali to the throne of the Carnatic, but had been circumvented at every turn, and were now called upon to acknowledge the superior authority of their bitter enemy Dupleix.

[Sidenote: Triumph of Robert Clive.]

British rule in Southern India was at its last gasp. If Dupleix could only have got hold of Mohammed Ali, he might have been master of the Carnatic; Madras might have been a French settlement, and a French Governor and Council might have taken the place of the British in Fort St. George. As it was, Mohammed Ali was very nearly surrendering. He had fled away to seek the help of the Hindu Rajas of the south and was being closely besieged by the French in the city of Trichinopoly, 180 miles to the south of Arcot. During this crisis, Robert Clive saved the East India Company. He left Madras with a small force, and after a march of seventy miles into the interior, threw himself into the city of Arcot, the capital of the Carnatic, where the Nawabs of the Carnatic had held their court for more than half a century. The native garrison fled at his approach, and the inhabitants, numbering 100,000, offered no resistance. The French were aghast at hearing that the capital of the Carnatic was in the hands of the British. They despatched a large force from Trichinopoly but failed to recover Arcot. In the end, they raised the siege of Trichinopoly, and Mohammed Ali was delivered out of their hands and placed by the British in possession of the Carnatic, to the exclusion of Dupleix and ruin of his ambitious schemes.

[Sidenote: Tragedy at Calcutta, 1756.]

British and French were now anxious for peace and agreed to make Dupleix their scapegoat. They threw the whole blame of the war upon the unfortunate Frenchman, who returned to France and died in poverty. In 1755 a treaty was patched up at Pondicherry but was never executed. In 1756, on the eve of the Seven Years' War, terrible news arrived from Bengal. The Nawab had captured the settlement at Calcutta, and a hundred and twenty-three English prisoners had been thrust into a barrack cell and perished most miserably of heat and suffocation.

[Sidenote: Threats of the Nawab of Bengal.]

§11. The tragedy was appalling, but the causes were intelligible. About the beginning of the eighteenth century, a Nawab of Bengal, Behar, and Orissa, territories considerably larger than the United Kingdom, had removed his capital from Dacca to Murshidabad, about a hundred miles due north of Calcutta. Here he founded a dynasty, which reigned in peace for some forty years. About 1742 a usurper seized the throne of Murshidabad and reigned as Nawab. He died of extreme old age in April 1756 and was succeeded by a grandson, a young man timid and suspicious, surrounded by foes eager to take his life and throne. The new Nawab heard that Governor Drake was sheltering one of his enemies at Calcutta, and strengthening the fortifications, and he ordered the British to surrender the refugee and stop further defenses. Governor Drake replied that he knew nothing of any enemies of the Nawab; that he was ready to obey the Nawab in all things; and that he was repairing the defenses on the river to prevent being surprised by the French, as Madras had been surprised ten years before. The Nawab was in a fury at this message and set off for Calcutta in the heats of June with an army of fifty thousand men.

[Sidenote: Defences at Calcutta.]

For half a century the British had paid little or no attention to their defenses. Fort William had been deemed sufficient protection on the side of the river, and on the land side the native inhabitants had begun to dig a ditch as a defense against the Mahratta horsemen, but the Mahrattas were paid chout to go away, and the ditch was never finished. The Europeans dwelt in houses and gardens along the bank of the river Hooghly, on either side of Fort William; and an English Church, the Mayor's Court, and some other buildings covered Fort William on the land side. The native quarter, including a large bazaar, adjoined the Mahratta ditch, and avenues of trees led from the native quarter to Fort William and the European buildings.

[Sidenote: Neglected precautions.]

Had Governor Drake or any member of his Council possessed a spark of military genius, they might have held Fort William against the Nawab despite his superior numbers. There was a garrison of two hundred European soldiers in the Fort. The European residents should have abandoned their houses on the river, and repaired to the Fort with their wives and children. The neighboring buildings should have been demolished to prevent the Nawab's troops from approaching under cover. The enemy should have been harassed with shells all day and sallies all night until the Nawab raised the siege. Moreover, the beginning of the southwest monsoon was daily expected. With it would come the ships of the season from Europe. Could the besieged have held out for ten days, they might have been rescued by the ships, just as Charnock and the factors were carried away from Hughly some seventy years before.

[Sidenote: Weak preparations.]

Whilst the Nawab's army was approaching Calcutta, the native population was flying _en masse_ to the neighboring villages. There was also a large population of Portuguese half-castes, which should have been left to do the same, as they would have been in no manner of danger. Unfortunately, two thousand of these black women and children were admitted into the Fort, and the overcrowding and confusion were fatal. Meanwhile, batteries and breastworks were constructed in the avenues leading to the Fort, in the wild hope of protecting the whole European quarter; but they were too far away to be supported by reinforcements from the European garrison.

[Sidenote: Siege of Fort William.]

At noon on Wednesday, the 16th of June, the Nawab's army poured into the settlement through the unfinished portion of the Mahratta ditch. They set fire to the native bazaar, and, after meeting obstinate resistance, they captured the batteries and breastworks in the avenues. The European gunners spiked their cannon and fell back upon the Fort, but the Nawab's artillerymen drilled the cannon and turned them round towards the Fort; whilst bodies of the Nawab's matchlock men occupied the buildings outside the Fort which ought to have been demolished, and opened fire upon the ramparts and bastions.

[Sidenote: Escape of women and children.]

The fighting lasted all Thursday and Friday. On Friday night the English ladies and children were placed on board the single ship which lay before the Fort. On Saturday the firing was hotter than ever. Hopeless efforts were made to place the Portuguese women and children on board the ship, but they would have been safer in the neighboring villages, for the overcrowding was such that many boats were sunk and numbers were drowned. Governor Drake, however, got on board, and the ship moved slowly down the river, leaving the British soldiers and others to their fate.

[Sidenote: Loss of Fort William.]

Throughout Saturday night the garrison fired rockets for recalling the ship. At sunrise, they waved flags, but without effect. A Mr. Holwell, a member of Council, was elected Governor in the room of Drake. But resistance was useless. The British soldiers broke into the arrack-room and got hopelessly intoxicated. Late in the afternoon, a mob of the Nawab's troops advanced to the Fort with ladders. In a few moments they were swarming over the walls, whilst the drunken European soldiers ran to the back of the Fort and broke down the gates leading to the river. But the Fort was closely environed by the Nawab's troops, and whilst some of the fugitives may have escaped to the boats or been drowned in the river, the bulk was brought back into the Fort as prisoners of war.

[Sidenote: Black Hole tragedy.]

By this time the Nawab had taken possession of Fort William but was disappointed at finding very little money and only a poor stock of merchandise. The season ships to Europe had carried off all the Indian exports to escape the southwest monsoon, and the ships from England were waiting for the monsoon to carry their European cargoes up the river. There were 146 prisoners, and no place of security except the barrack cell, known as the Black Hole, which rarely held more than two or three prisoners, and was only eighteen feet square. In this horrid hole they were driven with clubs and swords, and the next morning only twenty-three were taken out alive.

[Side note: the first period is over.]

The first act of the East India Company's rule came to an end in this manner.

The British traders quickly ushered in a new era of conquest and domination, but the catastrophe that occurred in Calcutta in June 1756 has never been forgotten, and to this day, no English person living in India does not occasionally bring up the traumatic memories of the Black Hole.

[6]

FOOTNOTES:

[1] Although they were technically under Mohammedan rule, the island of Goa and the citadel of Diu in Guzerat were independent and held by force.

[2] The authorities for the present chapter, which deals with the rise and early development of British rule in India, are somewhat numerous. The most important is the Government records at Madras, in which the weekly transactions of the Governor and Council are entered at full length in a series known as "Consultations." Every year a copy of the "Consultations" was sent to the Court of Directors, together with a summary of the affairs of the year as a "General Letter;" and every year a "General Letter" was received from the Court of Directors, reviewing the "Consultations," and conveying instructions and orders thereon. The Madras records have been closely investigated by the author from 1670 to 1748; and printed extracts were published at Madras in 1860-62, in three volumes small quarto, under the title of _Madras in the Olden Time_. To them may be added Bruce's _Annals of the East India Company_; Sir Thomas Roe's _Journal of a Mission to the Great Mogul_ in 1616-18; and the travels of Pietro Della Valle, Tavernier, Thevenot, and Fryer; as well as Orme's _History of Hindustan_, Stewart's _History of Bengal_, Faria y Souza's _History of Portuguese Asia_, and Shaw's _Predecessors of the High Court at Madras_. Further authorities will be found cited in the author's _History of India from the Earliest Ages_, and in his _Early Records of British India_.

[3] The Mofussil Courts, and the High Court in Appeals from the Mofussil Courts, are still required to decide, according to "equity and good conscience." See the "High Court amended Charters" granted in 1866.

[4] This was notoriously the case at Surat, where female slaves might be purchased by Europeans. There was a Dutch factory at Surat of the same stamp as the British factory, and its married inmates were in a like manner forbidden to bring their wives from Holland. But when the Dutch got possession of Java, they offered grants of land to married Dutchmen, and, according to Pietro Della Valle, there was a sudden change in domestic arrangements. Dutch bachelors were in such a hurry to go to Java, that they married Armenian Christians, or went off to the bazaar and bought female slaves and baptized them, and married them without loss of time.

[5] Abbé Dubois, who lived many years in Southern India, could not account for the distinction between the two Hands; Dr. Fryer was told about 1676 that the antagonism was planned by the Brahmans to keep the lower castes in subjection.

[6] Professor Terrien de Lacouperie has kindly noted that a distinction between the right and left hands has persisted in Central and Eastern Asia for a remote period since the previous chapter was written in type. Both before and during the Christian era, the Turkish Hiung-nu in northwest China had officers divided into two divisions: a left and a right side. The Burut-Kirghiz are still separated into two wings, the right-wing is called "on" and the left-wing "sol."

In China, the task of keeping a daily chronicle of "words" and "facts" was entrusted to two officers, one on the left hand of the emperor and the other on his right.

The officer on the left recorded all speeches and addresses, whilst that on the right recorded all facts and events. This last division, however, is a mere title in Chinese administration; the left hand being more honorable than the right and taking precedence.

It has previously been shown that the differentiation between the right and left hands in Southern India is a product of caste rivalry, thus it is impossible to determine whether or not it is related to the practices in Central Asia or China. The Dravidian populations of Southern India undoubtedly migrated from the area beyond the Himalayas at some unspecified point in time, but no historical connections are apparent other than linguistic evidence. In his lectures on "Indo-Chinese Philology," Professor Terrien de Lacouperie noted that the Dravidian group constitutes the fourth division of the Kueonlunic branch of Turanian languages.

9 798887 833842

Printed by Libri Plureos GmbH in Hamburg,
Germany